W9-AGM-932

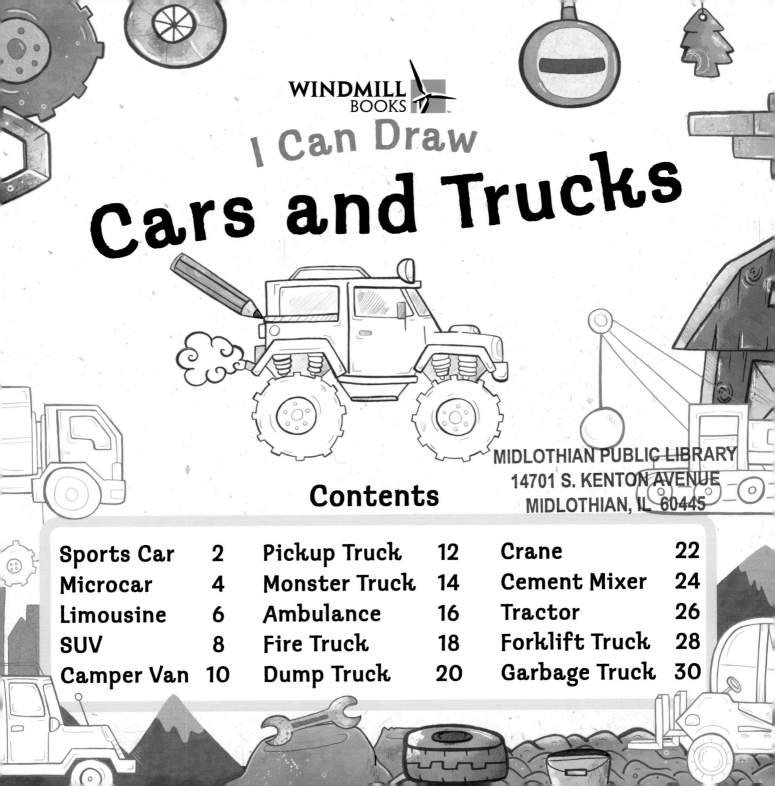

WINDMILL BOOKS

I Can Draw
Cars and Trucks

Contents

Sports Car	2	Pickup Truck	12	Crane	22
Microcar	4	Monster Truck	14	Cement Mixer	24
Limousine	6	Ambulance	16	Tractor	26
SUV	8	Fire Truck	18	Forklift Truck	28
Camper Van	10	Dump Truck	20	Garbage Truck	30

Sports Car

1. Draw two circles for the tires.

2. Pencil in the lower half of the car from the hood to the back end.

3. Add the roof.

4. Draw a door and two windows.

5. Pencil in lights and a fuel tank cap.

6. Add a mirror, side light, wheels, and detail to the door.

3

Microcar

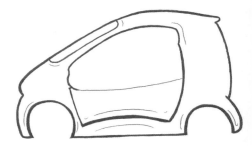

1. Carefully pencil the car's body shape.

2. Draw a door.

3. Draw the windshield. Add lines to the door.

4. Sketch in a headlight, rear window, and trunk.

5. Draw tires, side mirror, and badge.

6. Add the wheel arch, wheels, window, and door handle.

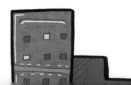

Limousine

1. Draw tires and wheels for the stretch limo.

2. Sketch the car's long chassis.

3. Pencil the car's outline from the hood to the trunk.

4. Add windows, a windshield, and front, side, and rear lights.

5. Draw front and rear doors, door handles, and a side mirror.

6. Sketch in the fuel tank cap, antenna, and a line between the wheels.

SUV

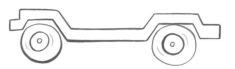

1. Draw two large tires and wheels.

2. Pencil in the chassis with its wheel arches and bumpers.

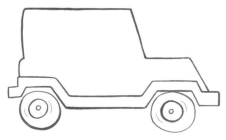

3. Sketch the SUV's boxy body.

4. Draw doors and windows. Add detail below the rear window.

5. Add a side mirror, headlight, grille, roof rack, and handles.

6. Add a spare wheel, antenna, and shading to the windows and panels.

Camper Van

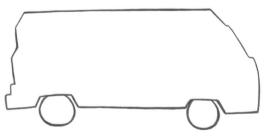

1. Draw two tires.

2. Pencil in the outline of the camper van's body and chassis.

3. Add three windows.

4. Draw the rear bumper and front door. Add roof and window details.

5. Draw hubcaps, a side door, and add detail to the panels.

6. Sketch a spare wheel, rear vent, handles, and fancy paintwork.

Pickup Truck

1. Draw two tires and wheels.

2. Sketch the chassis and wheel arches.

3. Draw the hood, cab, and bed of the truck.

4. Add a rear light, bumpers, and body trim.

5. Draw a window and side mirror.

6. Add a fuel cap, door handle, and side light.

Monster Truck

 1. Draw two large, chunky tread tires and wheels.

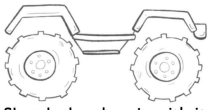

 2. Sketch the chassis with its high wheel arches.

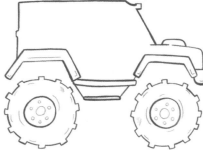

3. Draw the outline of the monster truck.

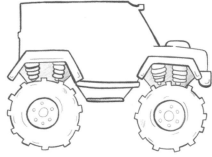

4. Sketch the suspension system between wheels and chassis.

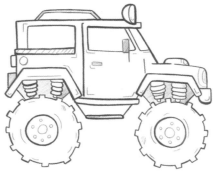

5. Add a door, handle, mirror, fuel cap, rack, lights, and windows.

6. Add an exhaust pipe and smoke, and window and panel details.

Ambulance

1. Draw tires, wheels, and the chassis.

2. Sketch the outline of the ambulance.

3. Pencil in a stripe along the side of the ambulance.

4. Draw a side mirror and a front window.

5. Pencil the rear door, window, and handle.

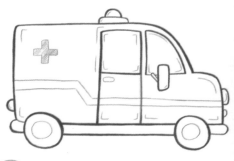

6. Add front, rear, and roof lights, and a cross.

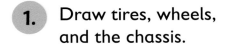

Fire Truck

1. Draw two tires and wheels.

2. Pencil in the chassis with its bumpers.

3. Draw the cab, windows, and door handle.

4. Add stripes, a hose and nozzle, dials, gauges, and a rear panel.

5. Draw the ladder and its mounting base.

6. Finish by adding the flashing light above the cab.

Dump Truck

1. Draw three tires and wheels.

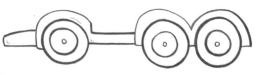

2. Sketch the chassis with its wheel arches and bumper.

3. Sketch the outline of the truck's cab.

4. Add the lights, side mirror, door, handle, and windows.

5. Pencil in the dump box and rear bumper.

6. Add panel details and rubble to the dump box.

Crane

1. Draw five tires and wheels.

2. Add two lines between each tire.

3. Draw the caterpillar track around the wheels.

4. Pencil in the crane's engine box and control cab.

5. Sketch a door, windows, and an antenna.

6. Draw the arm of the crane, a chain, and a wrecking ball.

Cement Mixer

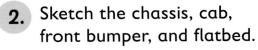

1. Draw three tires and wheels.

2. Sketch the chassis, cab, front bumper, and flatbed.

3. Add a window, door handle, and headlight.

4. Draw the mixer drum.

5. Pencil in two posts to support the mixer drum.

6. Add the exhaust pipe, roof light, and stripes to the drum and cab.

Tractor

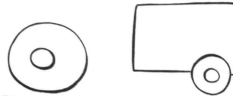

1. Draw a large and small tire and wheel.

2. Pencil in a rectangle, as shown, near the small wheel.

3. Sketch a wheel arch over the large wheel.

4. Draw the tractor's cab.

5. Add the steering wheel, driver's seat, and exhaust pipe.

6. Give the tires a chunky tread and add nuts to the wheels.

Forklift Truck

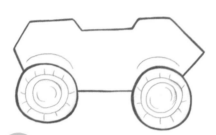

1. Draw two tires and wheels.

2. Draw the truck's chassis and body.

3. Sketch the cab.

4. Add the steering wheel and windows.

5. Draw the truck's lift system.

6. Add a cab door, light, forks, and panel details.

Garbage Truck

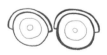

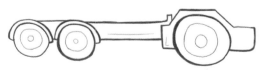

1. Draw two small wheels with arches and a large wheel.

2. Add the chassis, front wheel arch, and bumper.

3. Pencil in the outline of the cab.

4. Draw the waste cart and the rear hopper section.

5. Sketch the cab door and window, front lights, and bumper detail.

6. To finish, add panels and stripes to the cart and hopper.

Published in 2019 by Windmill Books,
an Imprint of Rosen Publishing
29 East 21st Street, New York, NY 10010

Created and Produced by Green Android Limited
Illustrations by Grace Sandford

Cataloging-in-Publication Data

Names: Sandford, Grace.
Title: I can draw cars and trucks / Grace Sandford.
Description: New York : Windmill Books, 2019. | Series: I can draw
Identifiers: ISBN 9781538390122 (pbk.) | ISBN 9781508197287 (library bound) | ISBN
9781538390139 (6 pack)
Subjects: LCSH: Automobiles in art--Juvenile literature. | Trucks in art--Juvenile literature. |
Drawing--Technique--Juvenile literature.
Classification: LCC NC825.A8 S264 2019 | DDC 743'.896292--dc23
Manufactured in the United States of America

CPSIA Compliance Information: Batch BW19WM: For Further Information contact Rosen Publishing,
New York, New York at 1-800-237-9932